Great
Papier Mâché

The Author would like to acknowledge the support of the School of Applied Arts and Design, De Montfort University, Lincoln, in the preparation of this book.

With thanks to Access students from De Montfort University for making the clocks featured on pages 5, 6, 7, 54 and 55.

With special thanks to Steve Price, and all my friends at Sunnybrook Farm for their help and support.

The Author and Publishers would like to thank Benedict, Charlotte, Daisy, Daniel, Emily, Lucia, Michael, Rupert and Samantha for posing so patiently for the photographs.

__Opposite:__ This distinctive stripy cat is made by applying paper pulp on to a wire frame; the bold decoration is made with torn sugar paper. Full step-by-step instructions showing how to make this striking cat are given on pages 31–36.

Great Papier Mâché

Masks ◆ Animals ◆ Hats ◆ Furniture

GERRY COPP

SEARCH PRESS

First published in Great Britain 1997

Search Press Limited
Wellwood, North Farm Road,
Tunbridge Wells, Kent TN2 3DR

Text copyright © Gerry Copp
Photographs by Search Press Studios

Photographs and design copyright © Search Press Ltd. 1997

Suppliers
If you have any difficulty in obtaining any of the materials and
equipment mentioned in this book, then please write for a current
list of stockists, including firms who operate a mail-order service, to
the Publishers.
Search Press Limited, Wellwood,
North Farm Road, Tunbridge Wells,
Kent TN2 3DR, England

ISBN 0 85532 815 0

Mermaid
by Sally Machin

*This attractive clock is made by
applying paper pulp on to a
cardboard base.*

Printed in Spain by Elkar S. Coop. Bilbao 48012

Contents

Introduction

If you want to develop the basic techniques of papier mâché and make things on a large scale, then *Great Papier Mâché* is the book for you. The masks, hats, animals and furniture featured in this book are theatrical, functional and fun. The various projects can be made by adults and children, individuals and groups, the complete beginner and those with more experience. In particular, some of the larger projects are ideal for group work, where many hands will make light work.

The introductory chapter gives advice on the safe use of materials and equipment, and where to find the items you will need. This chapter also describes the basic techniques involved in papier mâché; it is a good idea to familiarise yourself with these as they are frequently referred to during the projects. Lots of exciting projects follow, and clear step-by-step photographs and text will guide you through every stage – from using cardboard, wire netting and clay as bases, to decorating the papier mâché with coloured paper, photocopies and paint.

Please note that although aimed at both children and adults, some of the processes described in this book do require adult supervision.

Before you begin working through a project, it is worth spending a little time preparing for it. It helps to collect together all the materials and tools listed at the beginning of the project so that everything will be easily to hand whilst you are working. In addition to the materials listed, you will need a supply of water, and containers for things like paint and paste. You will find it helpful to read through the text and look at the photographs for the project before you begin – this will help you to gauge how much time each stage will require, and how long to allow for the papier mâché and paint to dry; you can then plan around this.

You may want to follow the detailed instructions for each project exactly, or you could adapt them to devise your own variations on the themes. Throughout the book, examples are shown of alternatives to the main projects which I hope will inspire you. Papier mâché is versatile and is suitable for a wide range of decorative treatments, so the possibilities are endless.

It may be hard to believe that inexpensive, everyday materials like cardboard and newspaper can be transformed into elaborate hats, quirky animals and functional furniture, but this book shows that they can be! Whatever you decide to make, papier mâché is great fun, and I hope you enjoy exploring the possibilities as much as I did when creating the projects that appear in this book.

Materials and tools

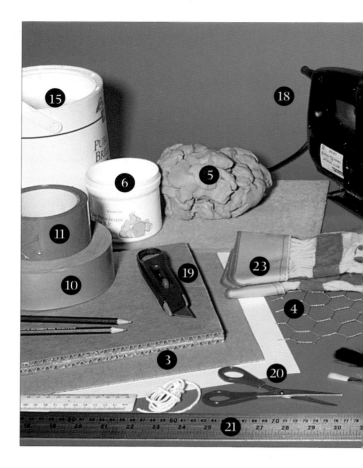

1. Paper for papier mâché

Newspaper is ideal for large scale papier mâché as it is inexpensive and easily obtainable. When it is dry, it must be sealed with white emulsion paint.

White waste paper should be used instead of newspaper if you do not intend to paint the dry papier mâché – for example, if you wish to decorate with collage.

2. Paper for decoration

Sugar paper is inexpensive, absorbent, ideal for collage on a three-dimensional surface, and is available in a range of colours. It does, however, have a tendency to fade over time.

Tissue paper is easy to use and can produce some interesting effects; it can be scrunched up, or a light colour can be layered over a darker one. It is available in a range of bright colours but, like sugar paper, it will fade over time.

3. Corrugated cardboard

Single (0.5cm, about ¼in thick) and double (1cm, about ½in thick) corrugated cardboard are used as supports for papier mâché. Single corrugated card is light and easily bent in the same direction as the corrugations. Double corrugated card is much more rigid and less likely to warp. Packaging and box manufacturers often supply cardboard; they can be contacted through telephone listings.

Paper and card are available in a variety of sizes. This book uses:

A1 (approximately 32 x 24in)
A2 (approximately 24 x 16in)
A4 (approximately 12 x 8in)

---

4. Galvanised wire mesh

Wire mesh can be cut and shaped to make robust and complex structures. It is available by the length or by the roll from DIY stores. The wire can be cut with old scissors or wire cutters. Wear safety glasses and protective gloves, and fold over cut ends as you work.

5. Clay

Modelling clays and other modelling materials are available from craft shops; most are suitable for use as moulds for papier mâché. Clay can be shaped and moulded into complex forms. It does not need to be fired or even dried before being covered with papier mâché.

6. Petroleum jelly

Petroleum jelly is used as a releasing agent to prevent papier mâché from sticking to a clay mould; it can leave the surface a bit greasy.

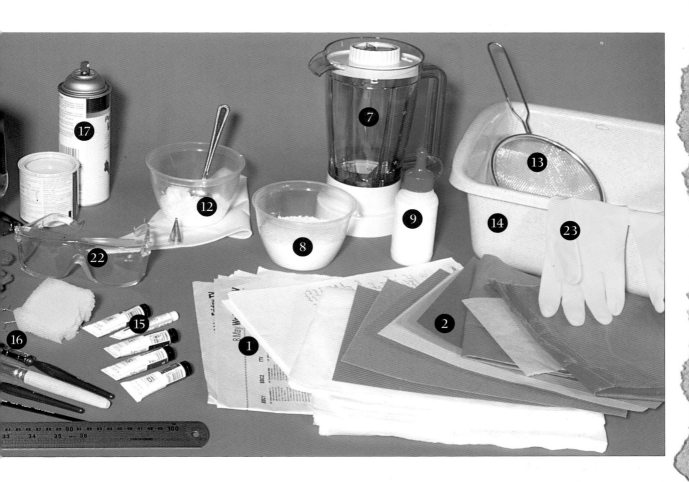

7. Liquidiser

A domestic food liquidiser is used to reduce paper to pulp for papier mâché. Always use a circuit breaker; never put your hand into the jug whilst it is attached to the base; never over-load or over-fill the jug; and do not run the motor for longer than recommended by the manufacturer.

8. Wallpaper paste

Wallpaper paste can be used with pulped and layered papier mâché. Most wallpaper pastes contain fungicide which can cause skin and eye irritation, so wear rubber gloves if you have sensitive skin. Always follow the manufacturers' recommendations. Non-toxic wallpaper paste, without fungicide, is available from toy shops, educational suppliers and some paint retailers. This paste is more suitable for children to use.

9. PVA glue

PVA (polyvinyl acetate) is a thick, white, water-soluble glue available from DIY stores and craft shops. It is very versatile and can be used for papier mâché, for collage, and as a sealant for interior filler.

10. Gum strip

Gum strip is a paper tape with gum on one side which becomes sticky when moistened. It does not lift away from card when it becomes damp, and papier mâché will stick to its paper backing. It is available from craft shops and stationers.

11. Plastic parcel tape

Plastic parcel tape is useful for securing cardboard quickly and firmly, but it should be removed and replaced with gum strip if papier mâché is to be applied over it.

12. Interior filler and piping bag

Interior filler is piped on to dry papier mâché to make relief patterns. It is best to have control over the consistency, so mix up the powder yourself rather than using ready-mixed filler. Mix in a plastic, glass or ceramic container and sieve well. When the piped filler has dried, it should be coated with PVA glue to seal it and to prevent it from chipping off.

13. Sieve

A sieve is used to remove lumps from interior filler, as these can block the nozzle of a piping bag.

14. Bowls

Plastic, glass or ceramic containers can be used for wallpaper paste and pulp.

15. Paints

Matt water-based white emulsion paint should be brushed over newspaper papier mâché to seal it. Watercolours, gouache and water-based acrylics are all suitable for decorating papier mâché and all these paints are available in a wide range of colours.

16. Paint brushes and sponges

Decorators' paint brushes can be used for applying white emulsion paint and paste. Finer artists' paint brushes and household sponges are suitable for applying paint for decoration.

17. Varnishes

Varnishing finished papier mâché objects protects them. For objects decorated with paper use a multi-purpose sealer, available from DIY shops, or a paper lacquer available from craft shops. If water-based paints have been used, use a spray varnish such as car spray lacquer. Always test a varnish before using it to make sure that it is compatible with the decorative finish you have used.

18. Saws

A jig-saw is an electrically powered tool which can be used for cutting double corrugated cardboard. It is easy to use, but you must follow the manufacturers' safety recommendations. It is sensible to always use a circuit breaker and to wear safety glasses. Jig-saws are for use by adults only; children should not use power tools.

A panel saw is a hand-held saw that can be used for cutting double corrugated cardboard. It will not cut as quickly as a jig-saw and it is much harder work to use. It is not a precision tool and so, for complex shapes, it should be used in conjunction with a craft knife.

19. Knives

Use a heavy duty craft knife with a retractable blade for cutting paper and cardboard. Scalpel-type knives are not suitable for cutting thick card. Always use a sharp blade and let this do the work – never force the knife to cut. Cut against a metal safety ruler or a solid raised edge. Keep your fingers well away from the line of the cut. Protect your work surface with a cutting mat or a piece of card.

20. Scissors

Paper and thin card can be cut with scissors. Old scissors or wire cutters can be used for cutting wire mesh.

21. Rulers

It is useful to have a 30cm (12in) metal safety ruler for cutting against, and a 100cm (36in) ruler for measuring with.

22. Safety glasses

Safety glasses are inexpensive and readily available from DIY shops. Always wear safety glasses when working with wire mesh and when using a jig-saw.

23. Protective gloves

Wear protective gloves when cutting wire mesh. Wear rubber gloves when applying paint with a sponge, to prevent your fingers from staining. If you have sensitive skin, wear rubber gloves when handling wallpaper paste.

Basic techniques

Using tools

Sharp knives and jig-saws should not be used by children. Adults using these tools should take all the necessary health and safety precautions, and should always follow the manufacturers' instructions. If in any doubt about safety, stop and seek advice. Do not use power tools if you are tired, as accidents are more likely to happen if concentration is poor.

Craft knife

Place the cardboard on a flat, solid surface protected by a cutting mat or a sheet of card. Use a metal safety ruler or a thick piece of wood to cut against. Keep your fingers well away from the cutting edge. Run the blade of a heavy duty craft knife against the side of the rule. Allow the blade to do the work and do not press too hard. Re-cut the same line several times if necessary.

Jig-saw

It is much easier to cut thick cardboard with a jig-saw rather than with a craft knife or a panel saw. Always use a circuit breaker when using a jig-saw, and always wear safety glasses. Work on a solid surface, preferably a work bench. Working away from the body, cut slowly and carefully. Allow the blade to do the work rather than trying to force the blade through the card. When cutting, always be aware of where your fingers and legs are and where the lead is at all times. Mark the card accurately, and always cut to leave the maximum amount of card to hold. When cutting large sheets of card you will need someone else to hold the card.

Using gum strip

1. Apply water to the shiny side of the gum strip using a damp sponge.

2. Join the two pieces of card with the gum strip and rub until smooth.

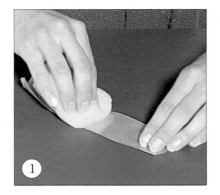 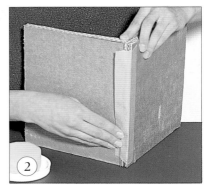

Layering using newspaper

1. Tear newspaper into small pieces. For large objects, use pieces up to a maximum size of about 10 x 20cm (4 x 8in). Very large pieces of pasted paper tend to lift as they dry.

2. Mix the wallpaper paste to a creamy consistency and smear it on to both sides of the paper.

3. Apply the newspaper to the cardboard, slightly overlapping the pieces of paper to cover the box. Rub over the paper with your fingers to press out any air bubbles and to make the surface smooth. Repeat to build up layers.

- **You can layer with white waste paper as well as with newspaper.**

- **Layered papier mâché takes about three or four days to dry at an average room temperature.**

12

Pulping using white waste paper

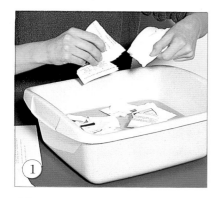

1 Tear the waste paper into small pieces. Soak the torn up paper in water for a few hours.

2 Fill the liquidiser with water and add a small handful of soaked paper.

3 Blend for ten to fifteen seconds, until the paper is reduced to a smooth pulp.

4 Pour the pulped paper from the liquidiser into a sieve to remove most of the water.

13

(5) Squeeze out the wet pulp until it is damp and no longer dripping.

(6) Rub the pulp between your fingers to break it up into small pieces.

(7) Add thick, but not sticky, wallpaper paste and squeeze it through the pulp to make a pliable, but not wet, mixture.

- **When squeezed into a column 5cm (2in) high, the pulp and paste mixture should remain upright.**

- **Adjust the quantities of pulp and paste to get the right consistency.**

- **Pulp takes about a week to dry at an average room temperature.**

Piping

Use approximately 150ml (5fl oz) of interior filler powder to 110ml (3½fl oz) of water. You can use a measuring jug to gauge the amount of interior filler. This quantity will make enough to fill a small piping bag. If you mix larger quantities, it tends to set hard before you can use it all. Wash all utensils immediately after use as the filler is very difficult to remove once it has set. Thorough sieving at various stages is important as lumps will block the nozzle and make piping impossible.

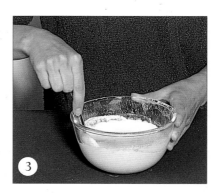

(1) Sieve the interior filler powder into a bowl.

(2) Re-sieve the powder into the water.

(3) Mix thoroughly.

14

④ Push the mixture through the sieve with the back of a spoon to remove any lumps.

⑤ Place the nozzle (No. 3 size) into the piping bag, then spoon the filler mix into the bag. Pipe patterns on to the dry papier mâché.

⑥ Allow up to an hour for the filler to dry. Brush over with PVA glue to seal the filler and prevent it from chipping off.

MASKS

Pirate mask

The lightness of papier mâché makes it the ideal material for large masks. The techniques shown in this section could be adapted to make all sorts of masks, and even costumes, for fancy dress, carnivals or theatrical performances. In this mask, the pirate's mouth serves as the hole for the eyes, so before you start you will need to establish the distance from your shoulder to your eye line. Adjust the position of the mouth or the depth of the collar as necessary. All the masks shown here have been decorated with sugar paper which is inexpensive and easy to use, but will fade in time. For longer lasting colour, you could use paint.

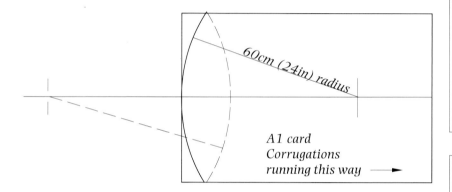

60cm (24in) radius

A1 card
Corrugations
running this way ⟶

You will need

A1 single corrugated card x 2
Pencil
Ruler
70cm (28in) string
Large pair of scissors
Craft knife
Brown parcel tape
Gum strip
Sponge
Wallpaper paste
Rubber gloves
White waste paper
Paint brush
Coloured sugar paper:
  A2 beige x 2, A2 black x 2,
  A2 red, A2 green,
  A4 white, A4 blue,
  A4 brown

It is important that the corrugations of the card run horizontal to the cut-out shapes.

① Draw a line down the middle of the length of the card, running in the same direction as the corrugations. Attach a pencil to the piece of string, leaving a final length of 60cm (24in). Place the pencil at one end of the centre line, and pull the string taut down the line. Holding the end of the string in place, plot an arc on the cardboard with the pencil. Repeat from the other side and then cut out the shape.

② Place the template on top of the card and draw round it. Repeat until you have eight shapes including the template. Cut out all the shapes.

Opposite: *These larger-than-life masks are made by applying layers of papier mâché on to a cardboard base. Using coloured sugar paper to decorate the masks, you can create a range of fun characters.*

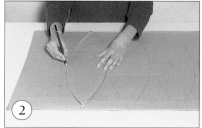

(3) Roll up each segment; this will make the cardboard easier to manipulate.

(4) Working on the inside, use short strips of parcel tape to join two segments together. Make a boat shape by pushing the edges together as the segments bend. Repeat until you have four pairs.

(5) Join two pairs of segments together using parcel tape on the inside of the seams. Repeat with the other two pairs.

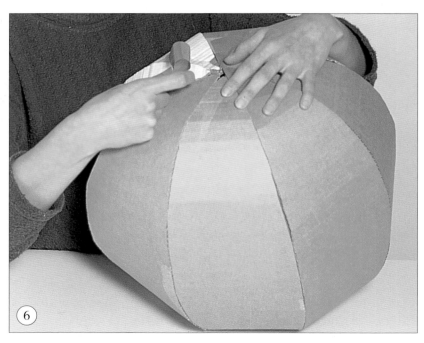

(6) Join the two halves together to make a ball. Secure the top and bottom with parcel tape. It helps to have a spare pair of hands for this step!

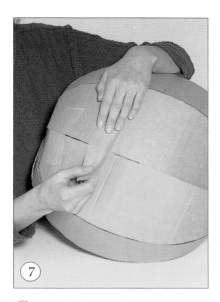

⑦ Work down the two open seams with short pieces of gum strip (see page 12). Remove the parcel tape at the bottom of the ball and replace with gum strip.

⑧ From the top of the ball, measure and mark approximately 9cm (3¹/₂in) down each seam. Cut along each seam with a craft knife down to the marked point, then open out the cardboard triangles.

⑨ Cut a strip of card 9cm x 70cm (3¹/₂in x 28in), with the corrugations running parallel to the width. Bend the card around the outside of the triangles to make the collar. Secure the points to the collar with gum strip.

⑩ Cover the mask and the collar with four layers of papier mâché (see page 12). Use white waste paper rather than newspaper. Leave to dry.

19

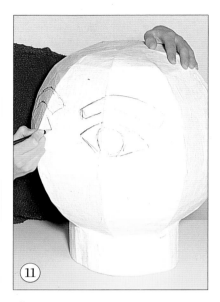

(11)

(12)

(13)

(11). Mark on the features using a pencil. The mouth should be about 20cm (8in) from the bottom of the collar, but this measurement will vary slightly, depending on your size (see page 17).

(12) Use scrunched up pieces of dry white paper to build up the eyes, nose and mouth. Tape the paper into position with gum strip.

(13) Build up the area around the eyes, nose and mouth using twisted pieces of dry paper. Use this technique to make the eyebrows as well.

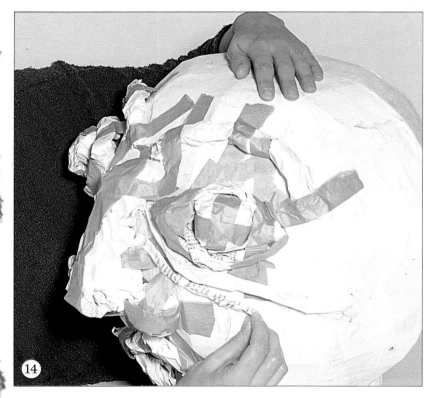

(14)

(14) Use thin strips of scrunched up pasted paper to build up finer features such as the moustache and face lines.

20

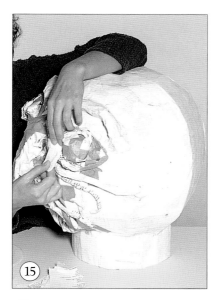

(15) Cover the features with three layers of papier mâché. When dry, use a craft knife to cut out the mouth.

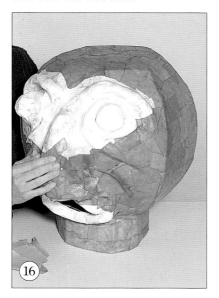

(16) Tear up beige sugar paper into small pieces. Smear each piece with wallpaper paste, and apply to the mask to give the overall skin colour.

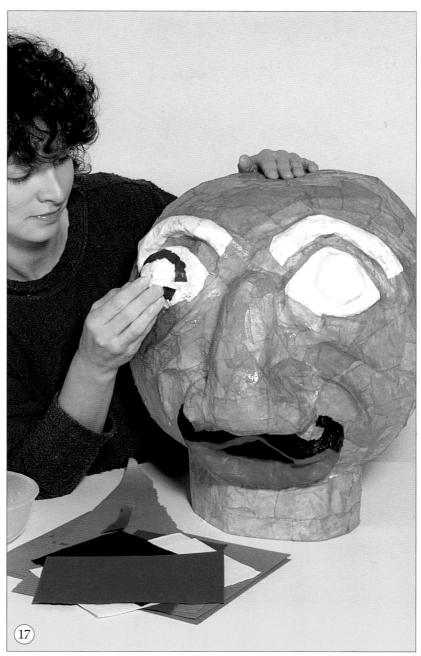

(17) Use pasted pieces of coloured sugar paper to cover the eyes, eyebrows, lips and moustache. For fiddly areas, use very small pieces of pasted paper. Rub the surface with your fingers until smooth.

21

19 Make the hair by tearing the black sugar paper into long strips. Smear the strips with wallpaper paste and scrunch lightly. Rub the crown of the head with wallpaper paste and apply the strands of hair.

18 To make the hat, tear red sugar paper into small squares and stick them on to an A2 sheet of green sugar paper using PVA glue. Leave to dry.

20 Brush the paper for the hat with wallpaper paste. Fold in the edges and position the hat on the head. Gather the paper in at the back and secure with a strip of black pasted sugar paper.

When dry, the mask can be varnished (see page 10) to make it more robust.

This stunning pirate mask is easy to make and is perfect for fancy dress, carnivals or theatre work. The mouth is designed to act as the hole for the eyes and the fact that it is made from paper and cardboard ensures that it is light and comfortable to wear.

These masks are made by applying papier mâché on to a clay base. Clay is very versatile, so try experimenting with it to create other exciting and colourful exotic birds.

Bird mask

These colourful and theatrical bird masks are not only ideal for fancy dress, carnivals and theatre work, but they also make wonderful decorative objects. Using clay as a base gives lots of flexibility for the shape of the mould and the papier mâché can either be cut away and the clay re-used, or the clay can be removed from the back of the mask. Craft and toy shops sell clay and other modelling materials. Before starting to make the mask, measure the distance from your chin to the level of your eyes, and measure the width of your face. Refer to these measurements when modelling the clay mould. Brightly coloured tissue paper and metallic pens have been used to decorate the masks in this section, but you could use other papers or paints.

<table>
<tr><td>You will need</td></tr>
<tr><td>A4 hardboard</td></tr>
<tr><td>Pencil</td></tr>
<tr><td>Clay</td></tr>
<tr><td>Small scraps of wood</td></tr>
<tr><td>Petroleum jelly</td></tr>
<tr><td>White waste paper</td></tr>
<tr><td>Gum strip</td></tr>
<tr><td>Wallpaper paste</td></tr>
<tr><td>Rubber gloves</td></tr>
<tr><td>Craft knife</td></tr>
<tr><td>Small, sharp scissors</td></tr>
<tr><td>Tissue paper in a range of colours</td></tr>
<tr><td>PVA glue</td></tr>
<tr><td>Paint brush</td></tr>
<tr><td>Metallic pens</td></tr>
<tr><td>Spray varnish</td></tr>
<tr><td>Ribbon</td></tr>
</table>

① Draw the shape of the mask on to the hardboard.

② Arrange the scraps of wood, which will act as a support for the clay, on to the hardboard; pay particular attention to the beak area. Build up the clay over the wood to make the overall shape and the features.

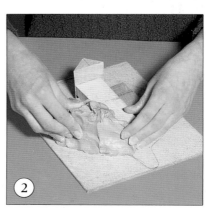

25

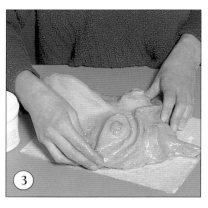

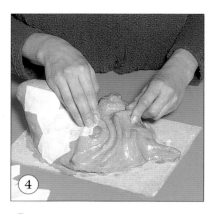

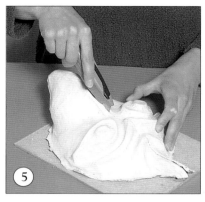

(3) Smear the surface of the clay mould with petroleum jelly.

(4) Apply eight layers of papier mâché (see page 12). Use white waste paper rather than newspaper. Leave to dry.

(5) Cut down the centre of the papier mâché mask with a craft knife (see page 11). Work slowly and carefully.

(6) Gently prise the two halves of the mask away from the clay mould.

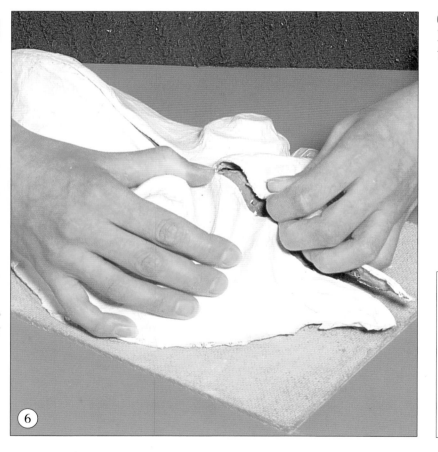

Following steps 5–7 will allow you to re-use the clay mould. If you do not want to save the mould, remove the hardboard from the back of the mask once the papier mâché is dry, and simply pull the clay out.

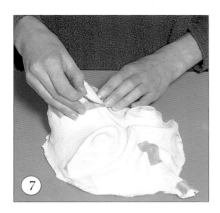

7

8

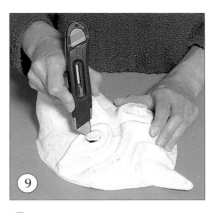

9

(7) Use small pieces of gum strip (see page 12) to join the two halves of the mask back together. Use white paper to papier mâché over the join and the inside of the mask. Leave to dry.

(8) Trim around the edge of the mask using a pair of small, sharp scissors.

(9) Carefully cut out the eye holes using a craft knife or a pair of scissors.

(10) Brush the mask with PVA glue mixed with a little water. Tear the tissue paper into small pieces and apply them to the mask. For stronger, richer colours, build up several layers. Brush over the tissue paper with the glue mixture.

10

11

(11) Tear the tissue paper into small shapes to make the more detailed decoration.

27

12 To make the ruffled texture around the beak and horn, use a strip of tissue paper about 2cm (³/₄in) wide. Brush glue on to the mask, gather the paper into place and glue in position. Allow to dry.

13 Use gold and silver metallic pens for the fine patterns. Spray with several coats of varnish (see page 10). Follow the manufacturers' instructions for both products.

14 Carefully make a small slit on each side of the mask using a craft knife. Thread ribbon through each slit and secure with a knot.

Papier mâché is applied to a clay base to create this stunning bird mask. Decorated with tissue paper and metallic pens, the result is vibrant and colourful. Try using paints in place of tissue paper for a different effect.

ANIMALS

This stripy cat is a real character. Paper pulp is applied to a wire frame, and the stunning colours and wonderful expression are created simply from torn sugar paper.

Stripy cat

For robust and complex structures, wire mesh is the ideal support for papier mâché. By cutting the wire into precise shapes, almost like a dressmaker working from a pattern, the wire can be manipulated into intricate forms. When using wire mesh, you should always wear protective gloves and safety glasses, and you should fold over cut ends as you work. If you want to make large structures, like the camel on page 38, it is important that the wire frame is sturdy, otherwise the weight of the wet papier mâché pulp will make it collapse.

You will need

120 x 60cm (48 x 24in) galvanised wire netting; 2.5cm (1in) mesh size

A2 tissue paper x 2

Protective gloves

Wire cutters/old scissors

Safety glasses

Ruler

White waste paper

Liquidiser

Sieve

Plate

Wallpaper paste

PVA glue

Paint brush for glue

Coloured sugar paper:
  A2 blue x 2,
  A2 orange, A4 black

Varnish

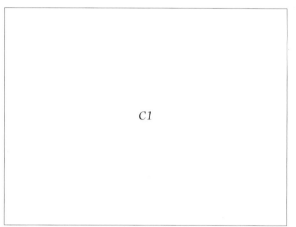
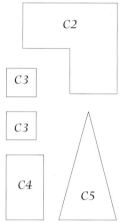

C1   *75 x 60cm (30 x 24in)*
C2   *25 x 25cm (10 x 10in)*
C3   *8 x 8cm (3 x 3in)* ***x 2***
C4   *10 x 18cm (4 x 7in)*
C5   *15 x 30cm (6 x 12in)*

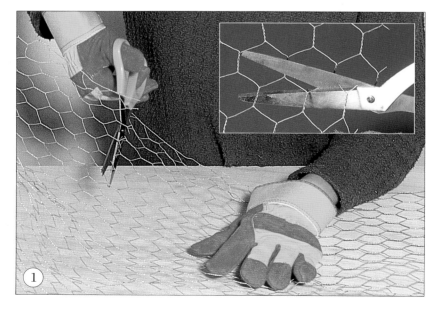

(1) Using the diagram as a guide, cut out the shapes from the wire mesh. Make sure that you cut through the single strands of wire, rather than the double twisted ones.

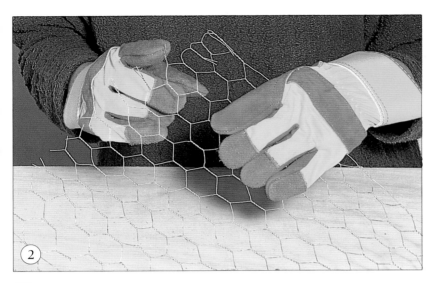

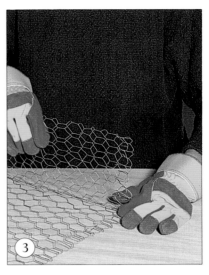

② Fold in the cut ends of the wire.

③ Fold piece C1 into four, so that you are left with a 75 x 15cm (30 x 6in) strip. Secure it by twisting a few of the cut ends of wire through the layers of netting.

④ Bend the strip 20cm (8in) from each end to form two right angles. Cut up the middle of both folded pieces to make the legs.

⑤ Pull the layers of mesh away from each other to form cylinders. Twist the cut ends through the adjoining wire to secure the shape.

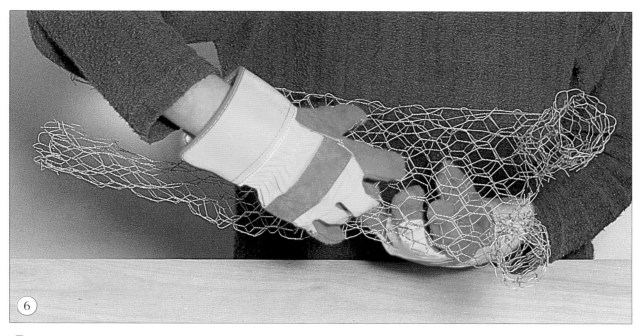

(6) With the legs fully extended, pull the layers of wire apart to form the body. Bend the legs back into position, and manipulate the wire until you are happy with the shape.

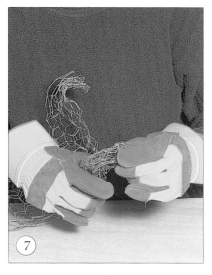

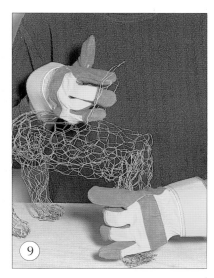

(7) Bend over the end of each leg to form the paws.

(8) Fold piece C2 so that the centre becomes the point of a ball. Squash gently to make the shape of the cat's head.

(9) Snip through the top layer of wire at the front end of the body to form the back of the neck. You will need to cut along the front, and about a third of the way down each side. Lift and stretch the cut piece of wire.

33

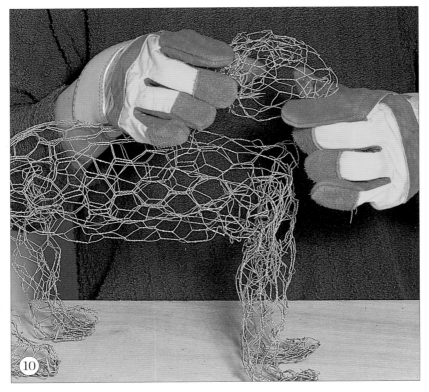

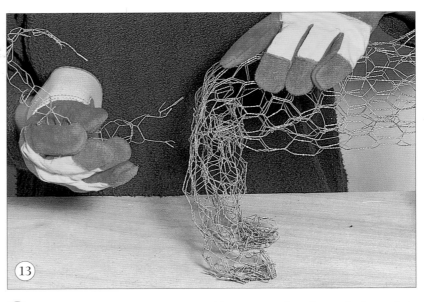

(11) Insert strip C4 under the head. Twist the ends of the cut wire into the head and the body. Twist the head into position. Squeeze and pull the wire to re-shape as necessary.

(10) To join the head to the body, twist the ends of the cut strip into the back of the wire head.

(12) To make the cat's ears, attach pieces C3 to the head by twisting in the cut ends. Squeeze the top of each square to form a point.

(13) Wrap piece C5 into a cone shape to make the tail. Attach it to the body, and then bend it to shape.

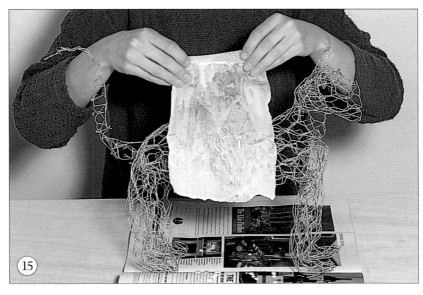

(14) Tear tissue paper into pieces approximately 10 x 15cm (4 x 6in). Dip each piece into a $^{50}/_{50}$ mixture of PVA glue and water, then drag up the side of the plate to remove excess glue.

(15) Drape the PVA-covered tissue paper over the wire. Cover the whole wire frame. Allow to dry.

(16) Cover the cat with pulp (see pages 13–14) by pressing the pulp gently on to the paper-covered frame and rubbing until smooth. The pulp should be about 0.5cm ($^1/_4$in) thick. You may have to apply the pulp in several stages as the weight of wet pulp can distort the frame. Allow to dry.

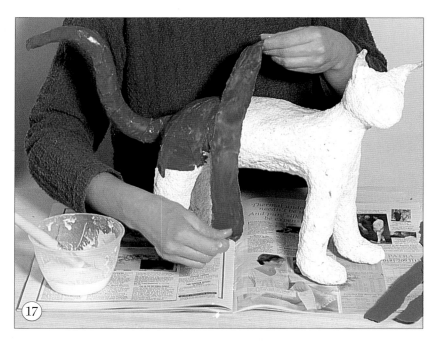

17 Brush the $^{50}/_{50}$ PVA and water mixture on to the pulp-covered frame. Tear the blue sugar paper into strips. Brush each strip with the glue mixture and apply to the cat. Rub the paper to make it smooth. Continue until you have covered the whole cat.

18 Tear the orange sugar paper into strips. Brush with the PVA and water mixture and stick down to form stripes.

19 Use torn coloured sugar paper to add the details such as the whiskers, eyes, ears and claws. Varnish the model (see page 10) to protect it.

36

Using the techniques shown in this chapter, you can create a whole range of unusual and striking cats.

The camel and giraffe shown here are both made using the same techniques as for the stripy cat, but instead of being decorated with sugar paper, they are painted with water-based acrylics. When making large objects like these, apply the pulp in stages, allowing each section to dry before applying the next. This will prevent the wire frame from collapsing under the weight of the wet paper pulp.

HATS

Princess's hat

The rich, textural finish of the princess's hat is achieved by piping interior filler (see pages 14–15) on to the papier mâché, and using a sponge to apply the paint.

By adapting the techniques described in this section, and combining them with others shown elsewhere in this book, you could make a hat for any occasion. The hats at the end of this chapter might give you some more ideas of what is possible.

(1) Lay out five sheets of tabloid-size newspaper. Slightly overlap each sheet then tape them together with gum strip (see page 12). Repeat until you have three long strips in total.

(2) Secure the end of one of the newspaper strips and then gently scrunch and twist to make a 'rope'. Repeat with the other two strips.

Opposite: These magical hats are made simply from thin card and newspaper. The addition of gold paint makes them look really luxurious – fit for a real princess.

You will need
Tabloid newspapers
Gum strip
A2 thin white card x 2
70cm (28in) string
Pencil
Scissors
Wallpaper paste
Rubber gloves
Interior filler
Piping bag and nozzle
Sieve
Spoon
PVA glue
Paint brushes
Sponge
White emulsion paint
Gouache:
   white
   ultramarine
   Prussian blue
   rich gold
Spray varnish

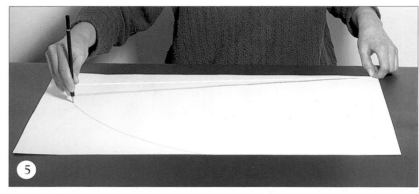

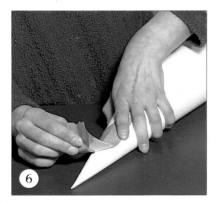

(4) Bind both ends of the plait with gum strip.

(3) Plait the three ropes together. You may need to twist the ropes as you work. The plait should be firm, but not tight.

(5) Attach a pencil to the string to leave a length of 60cm (24in). Hold the end of the string at one corner of the card, pull it taut with the pencil and plot an arc on to the card. Repeat on a second sheet of card.

(6) Cut along the pencil line, then bend to form a cone. Stick in place with gum strip.

(7) Place the cone on your head and adjust to the right size. Secure with gum strip. Make the second cone to fit inside the first; this will strengthen the hat.

42

(8) Bend the plait around the cone. Overlap the ends of the plait and secure them with gum strip.

(9) Remove the cone from the plait. Tear newspaper into strips approximately 8cm (3in) wide and use them to bind the plait. Join the pieces of newspaper with gum strip as you work.

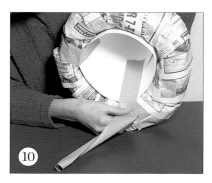

(10) Attach a length of gum strip to the inside of the cone.

(11) Bring the gum strip up over the ring and on to the outside of the cone.

(12) Apply four layers of papier mâché (see page 12), to the inside and outside of the ring, the outside of the cone and also a little way up the inside of the cone. Leave to dry.

(13) Spoon interior filler into a piping bag (see pages 14–15), and pipe patterns on to the cone and rim.

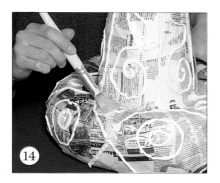

(14) When the filler is dry, brush over with PVA glue.

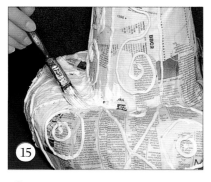

(15) When the glue is dry, paint the hat with white emulsion.

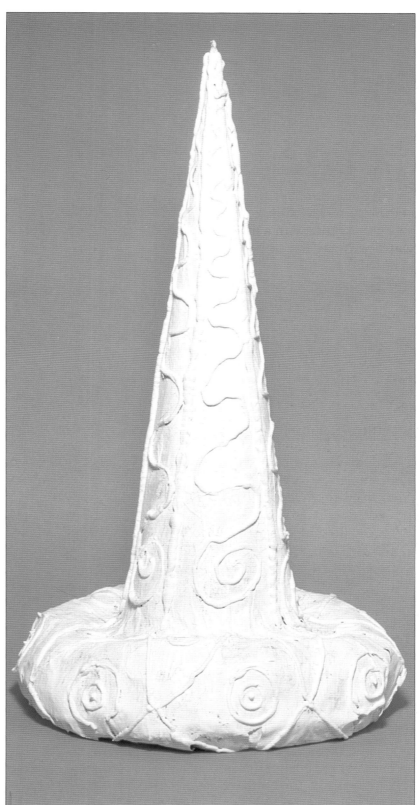

(16) Mix white and ultra-marine gouache to make a pale blue. Dilute with a little water and brush roughly on to the hat.

(17) Sponge on the Prussian blue gouache, varying the pressure to give a textural effect. Wear rubber gloves when you do this or your hands will stain.

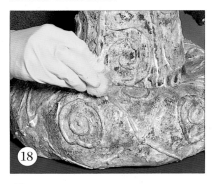

(18) Sponge the gold gouache on to the raised filler patterns. When dry, spray the hat with varnish (see page 10).

Finished with a beautiful textural design and luxurious gold paint, the princess's hat is dazzling. Try experimenting when piping the interior filler to create lots of different patterns.

You can adapt the techniques shown in this section to make a wide range of different hats – perfect for fancy dress, carnivals or theatre work.

47

Furniture

This fully-functional grandfather clock is made by applying layers of papier mâché on to double corrugated cardboard. It is painted and then decorated with photocopies of fish and shells which are carefully cut out and stuck on. You could use photocopies of any images, and if you like, you could apply a very thin wash of paint over them to give another splash of colour.

Grandfather clock

Made from corrugated card and papier mâché, this working grandfather clock is simple to make. A wide range of clock movements are available from craft shops and specialist suppliers (listed in telephone directories). This finished clock face is 25cm (10in) square, so the maximum length for the hands is 12cm (4¾in).

Before you can follow the step-by-step instructions for making this clock, you will need to draw all the pieces shown in the diagram on to double corrugated card (see page 8). Label all the pieces so that you will be able to identify them as you are working. Use a jig-saw to cut out the pieces (see page 11). At this stage, for pieces T1, T2, M1, B1 and B2, just cut out the basic rectangle shapes. Measure 15cm (6in) up from the bottom of one of the T1 pieces and cut out a 15cm (6in) square. Measure 5cm (2in) up from the bottom of the second T1 piece and cut out a 25cm (10in) square. Both these squares can be discarded. When you have cut out all the basic shapes, put pieces T3 and T4 aside. With the rest of the pieces, construct the three separate box sections using gum strip (see page 12).

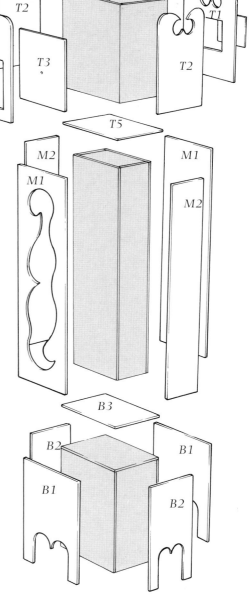

You will need

3m² (10ft²) double corrugated card

A1 thin card

Jig-saw (or panel saw or craft knife)

Safety glasses

Pencil

Ruler

Gum strip

Sponge

Newspaper

Wallpaper paste

Rubber gloves

Bottle cork

White emulsion paint

Paint brushes

Black coloured pencil

Photocopied pictures of fish and shells

Scissors

PVA glue

Gouache:
  cadmium yellow
  Prussian blue

Screwdriver

Epoxy resin

Pea stick 35cm (14in)

Spray varnish

Clock movement

All measurements are based on using double corrugated (1cm, ½in thick) card. They will need to be adjusted if a different thickness of card is used.

T1	35 x 46cm (14 x 18in) **x 2**
T2	23 x 46cm (9 x 18in) **x 2**
T3	33 x 35cm (13 x 14in)
T4	14.5 x 14.5cm (5¾ x 5¾in)
T5	35 x 25cm (14 x 10in)
M1	30 x 100cm (12 x 40in) **x 2**
M2	17 x 100cm (7 x 40in) **x 2**
B1	35 x 50cm (14 x 20in) **x 2**
B2	23 x 50cm (9 x 20in) **x 2**
B3	35 x 25cm (14 x 10in)

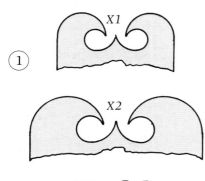

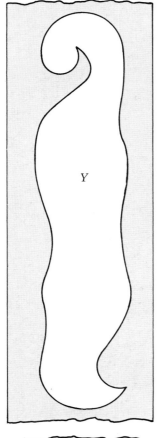

① Enlarge shapes X1, X2, Y, Z1 and Z2 on a photocopier and then trace them on to a piece of thin card to produce templates. You could draw them freehand straight on to thin card if you feel confident, or you could design your own decorative shapes.

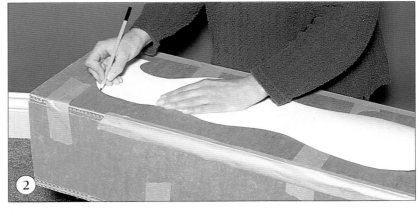

② Position template Y centrally on the front of the middle box section then draw around it.

③ Use a screwdriver to gouge a hole on the inside of the drawn line.

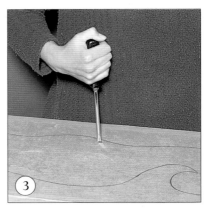

④ Put the jig-saw blade into the hole and cut along the line. Take all safety precautions and work slowly and carefully.

Now cut out the shapes from the top and bottom sections of the clock, working from templates X1, X2, Z1 and Z2.

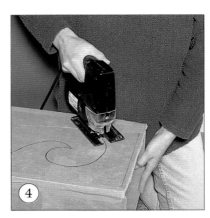

(5) Position the middle section centrally on top of the bottom section and attach it using gum strip along the joins. Secure the top section in the same way.

(6) Use a screwdriver to make a hole in the clock face (piece T3) as shown in the diagram on page 49. Slide the clock face into the front of the top section and tape into position on the inside.

(7) Apply five layers of papier mâché (see page 12) to the whole clock, including the inside of the middle section. Use strips of paper to bind the cut edges and to stretch across the inside of the legs. Build up a few extra layers on the joins to strengthen them. Cut a bottle cork in half and glue to the door (piece T4) using epoxy resin. Papier mâché over the top. Allow all the papier mâché to dry.

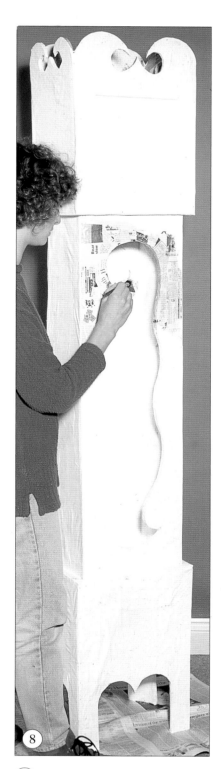

(8) Paint on the white emulsion to cover all the newspaper. Allow to dry.

51

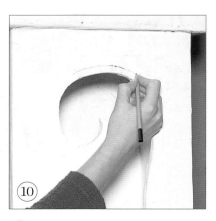

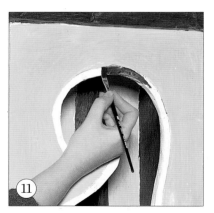

(9) Divide the sides, back, and inside of the middle section into stripes of equal width. The stripes on the inside will be slightly narrower than those on the outside. Draw on the lines with a black pencil – to prevent the clock from being pushed over whilst you do this, stand it against a wall or ask someone to hold it.

(10) Draw a line approximately 1.5cm (1/2in) from the edge of the front opening. To get an even line, hold the pencil as you would to write and push your middle finger against the edge of the card.

(11) Using cadmium yellow and Prussian blue gouache, paint the top section of the clock blue with a yellow face; paint the front of the middle section yellow, edge the front opening with blue, and paint blue and yellow stripes on the sides, back and inside; paint the bottom section blue. Allow to dry.

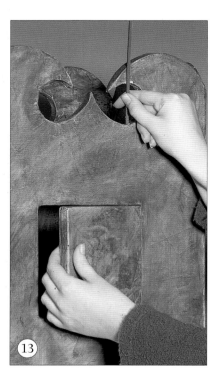

(12) Wearing rubber gloves, rub the paint with a damp sponge to distress the surface. You can rub quite vigorously, but take care not to rub over the line and mix the two colours. Use a clean piece of sponge for each colour.

(13) Working from the back of the clock, hold the door in position. Push a pea stick into the card and through the door. Trim off any excess stick.

52

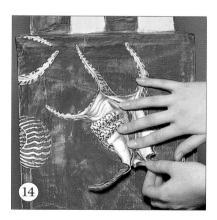

(14) Cut out photocopied pictures and stick them on to the clock using PVA glue.

(15) Push a screwdriver from the inside of the clock face into the hole previously made, to pierce through the papier mâché. Glue photocopies of small shells or other images on to the face to serve as 'numbers'. Position the 3, 6, 9 and 12 first.

Clock movements vary in size, weight and price and are available with and without pendulums. Ask suppliers for advice on selecting and installing movements.

(16) Apply several coats of spray varnish (see page 10). When dry, insert the clock movement following the manufacturer's instructions. If the movement is heavy it may need additional support inside the clock case. When the movement is in place, push the hands on to the spindle.

Bathers
Sally Machin

Punch and Judy
Penny McNeish

Starfish
Monika Leaman

These colourful clocks were made by adult students on an Access course. They all follow the theme of the seaside, and all use basic papier mâché techniques shown in this book. They have been decorated with paint and collage.

54

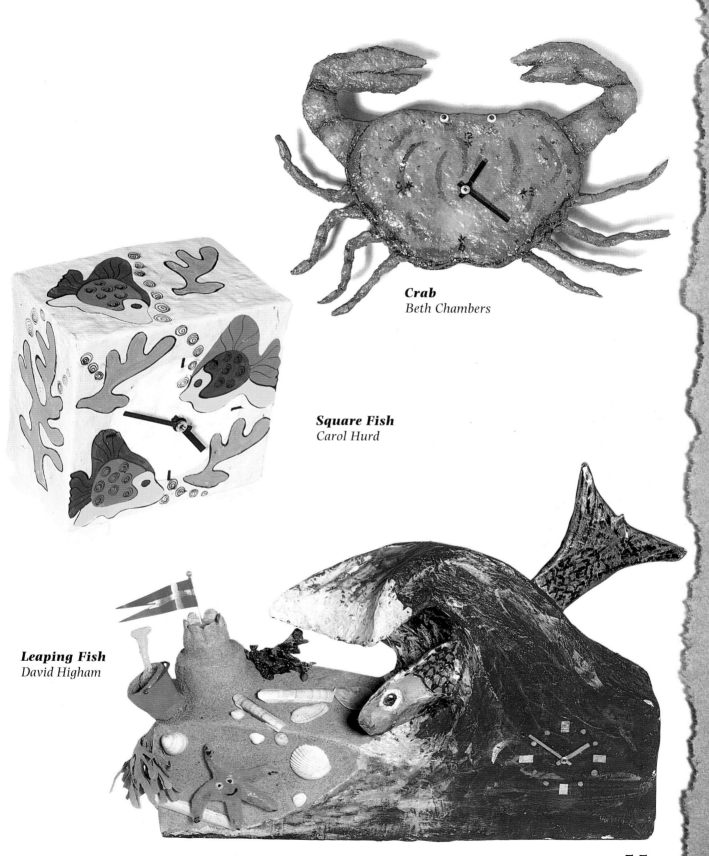

Crab
Beth Chambers

Square Fish
Carol Hurd

Leaping Fish
David Higham

55

Royal throne

Built from cardboard and newspaper, this throne is strong enough to support an adult, despite its light weight. You could make a variety of sturdy and functional pieces of furniture by using the structural and decorative ideas in this section.

Before you start to follow the step-by-step instructions for making the throne, draw all the shapes shown in the diagrams on this page and on pages 58, 59 and 60, on to double corrugated cardboard (see page 8). Cut out the pieces using a jig-saw (see page 11). When cutting out pieces T8, ensure that the corrugations run parallel to the length of the shapes.

Write the number shown in the diagram on each piece as you cut it out so that you can identify everything when constructing the throne. You cut the angles for pieces D1 at step 5, so at this stage simply cut out the basic rectangle shapes.

> **All measurements are based on using double corrugated (1cm, ¹/₂in thick) card. They will need to be adjusted if a different thickness of card is used.**

You will need

8m² (26¹/₂ft²) double corrugated card

Jig-saw (or panel saw, or craft knife)

Safety glasses

Pencil

Ruler

Gum strip

Craft knife

Sponge

Newspaper

Wallpaper paste

Rubber gloves

Interior filler

Piping bag and nozzle

Sieve

Spoon

PVA glue

White emulsion

Paint brushes

Gouache paint:
  spectrum violet
  brilliant violet
  rich gold

Spray varnish

T1	*60 x 40cm (24 x 15¹/₂in)*
T2	*60 x 135cm (24 x 53¹/₄in)*
T3	*60 x 100cm (24 x 39¹/₂in)*
T4	*58 x 29cm (23 x 11¹/₄in)*
T5	*58 x 45cm (23 x 17¹/₂in)* **x 2**
T6	*41 x 75cm (16 x 29¹/₄in)* **x 2**
T7	*58 x 41cm (23 x 16in)*
T8	*15 x 45cm (6 x 17¹/₂in)* **x 12**
T9	*60 x 41cm (24 x 16in)*

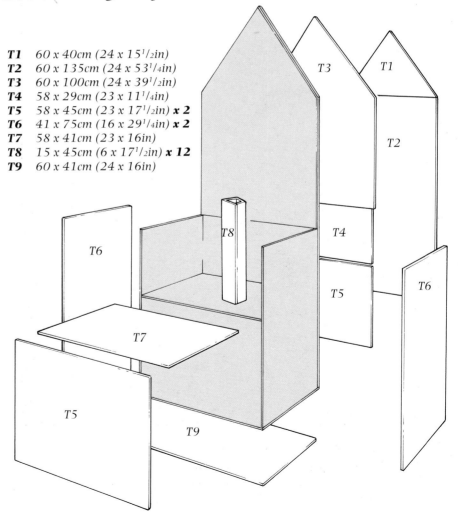

② Score pieces T8 with a craft knife and bend to form the tubular seat supports. Secure with gum strip and then position the supports in the base of the throne.

③ Pack scrunched up newspaper in and around each support in the base. Secure the seat (T7) on top of the supports using gum strip.

① Using the diagram as a guide, construct the basic structure of the throne by joining together the base (T9), sides (T6) and back (T1–T5) with gum strip (see page 12). Leave a 1cm (1/2in) gap between pieces T4 and T5.

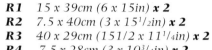

R1   15 x 39cm (6 x 15in) **x 2**
R2   7.5 x 40cm (3 x 15¹/₂in) **x 2**
R3   40 x 29cm (15¹/2 x 11¹/₄in) **x 2**
R4   7.5 x 28cm (3 x 10³/₄in) **x 2**

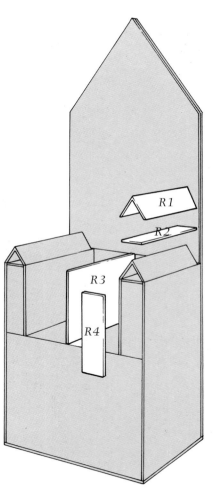

④ Construct the arms by scoring and bending the top of pieces R1. Assemble all the pieces as shown in the diagram. There should be a 1cm (¹/₂in) gap between the top of each arm and the back of the chair. When in position, secure all the pieces with gum strip.

58

D1 7.5 x 60cm (3 x 24in) **x 2**
D2 12cm (5in) diameter
D3 7.5 x 59cm (3 x 24in) **x 2**
D4 7.5 x 45cm (3 x 18in) **x 2**
D5 30 x 30cm (12 x 12in)
D6 7.5 x 60cm (3 x 24in) **x 4**
D7 7.5 x 10cm (3 x 4in) **x 4**
D8 7.5 x 28cm (3 x 11in) **x 2**
D9 7.5 x 30cm (3 x 12in) **x 2**

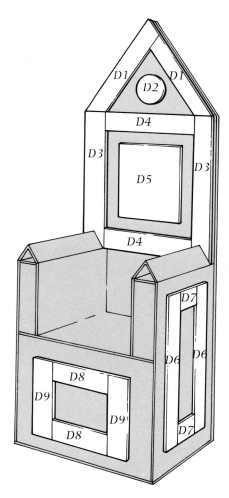

(5) Position the decorative panelling (D6–D9) as shown in the diagram and then tape in place. Position and attach strips D3 on the back of the throne, slotting them in behind the arms. Add strips D4 and panel D5. Hold strips D1 in place and use a ruler and pencil to mark the angles at each end. Cut to fit then tape in place. Position and secure the circular panel D2.

59

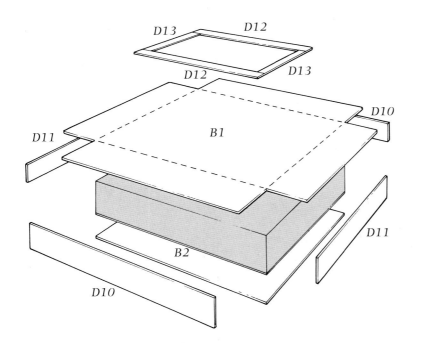

B1   110 x 90cm (44 x 36in)
B2   80 x 60cm (32 x 24in)
D10 8 x 82cm (3 x 33in) **x 2**
D11 8 x 60cm (3 x 24in) **x 2**
D12 4 x 72cm (1$^{1}/_{2}$ x 28$^{1}/_{2}$in) **x 2**
D13 4 x 45cm (1$^{1}/_{2}$ x 17$^{1}/_{2}$in) **x 2**

(6) Assemble the base by scoring an 80 x 60cm (32 x 24in) rectangle on the inside of piece B1. Cut square corners out, fold down the flaps and then attach to B2 using gum strip. Using the diagram as a guide, position the decorative strips (D10–D13) and then tape in place.

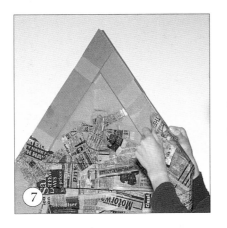

(7) Apply five layers of papier mâché (see page 12) to the throne and the base. Build up a few extra layers over the joins to strengthen them. You will need to wait until the top of the throne and the base are dry before applying papier mâché to the undersides of each. Leave everything to dry.

(8) Spoon interior filler into a piping bag (see pages 14–15) and pipe patterns on to the throne and base. Allow to dry then brush over with PVA glue.

(9) Paint the throne and base with white emulsion paint.

(10) Dilute the spectrum violet gouache with a little water and brush roughly on to the throne and base.

(11) Sponge on the brilliant violet gouache. Wear rubber gloves to prevent your hands from staining.

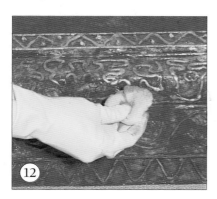

(12) Sponge the gold gouache on to the piped patterns. Allow to dry and then spray with varnish (see page 10).

(13) Carefully place the throne on the base.

Papier mâché is applied in layers on to a double corrugated card base to make this impressive throne. The elaborate piped pattern and the regal purple and rich gold paint make it perfect for any royal occasion. Using the techniques shown in this section, you could create a whole range of functional furniture.

Index

The author, aged four, experimenting with papier mâché.